# LIKE MUM USED TO MAKE

A collection of delicious easy-to-make recipes

## Contents

| | |
|---|---|
| Breakfast | 1 |
| Comfort Food | 11 |
| Tea Time | 29 |
| Sunday Roast | 43 |
| Puddings | 53 |
| Sauces | 69 |
| My Mum's Recipes | 81 |
| Index | 91 |

All rights reserved.

No part of this publication may be reproduced, stored in a retrieval system or transmitted by any means (electronic, mechanical, photocopying or otherwise) without the prior permission of the publisher.

Text by Alan Charles.

Originally published in 2009 by L&K Designs. This edition published in 2010 by Myriad Books Limited.

© L&K Designs 2009
Printed in China

*Publisher's Disclaimer*

The recipes contained in this book are passed on in good faith but the publisher cannot be held responsible for any adverse results. Please be aware that certain recipes may contain nuts.

# Breakfast

## Fried Eggs
Preparation time: 5 minutes
Makes 2

### Ingredients
2 eggs
3 tablespoons butter or oil
salt & white pepper to taste

### Preparation
1. Add the butter or oil (or mixture of both) to a frying pan on a medium heat.

2. Carefully crack the egg into the frying pan. Cook gently, basting the yolk with oil (using a teaspoon).

3. Cook until the white of the egg is fully set, but the yolk is still 'runny', or cook for a longer time if you prefer a set yolk.

4. If you prefer your eggs turned over, cook for about 2 minutes - use a spatula to turn the egg over, and cook for a further 2 minutes.

## Boiled Eggs
Preparation time: Up to 12 minutes

### Cooking times
2-3.5 minutes for soft boiled
3.5-4.5 minutes for medium soft
10-12 minutes for hard boiled

### Preparation
Drop eggs into boiling water and boil.

## Scrambled Eggs

Preparation time: 10 minutes
Serves 3-4

### Ingredients

6 eggs
6 tablespoons cream or milk
3 tablespoons butter
salt & white pepper to taste

### Preparation

1. Crack the eggs in a bowl and lightly beat them until they turn a consistent colour, then stir in the cream (or milk), season with salt and pepper.

2. Melt the butter in a saucepan over a medium heat.

3. Pour in the egg mixture, stir constantly until the eggs begin to thicken.

4. Reduce the heat and continue cooking until the eggs are set to the desired degree.

### Serving Suggestion

Serve on hot buttered toast.

## Breakfast

## *Coggled Eggs*

Preparation time: 5 minutes
Serves 2

### Ingredients

4 eggs
4 rashers bacon
50g (2oz) grated cheddar cheese
4 slices bread & butter

### Preparation

1. Dice the bacon, then place into the dish you will be eating from.

2. Crack eggs over bacon and cover with cheese. Cover bowl and place in microwave. Cook for 3 minutes in microwave.

### Serving Suggestion

Serve with buttered soldiers.

## *Omelette With Crispy Bacon*

Preparation time: 15 minutes
Serves 1-2

### Ingredients

1/2 tablespoon butter
3 eggs
1 tablespoon milk
2 rashers of streaky smoked bacon

### Preparation

1. Over a medium heat, melt the butter in an omelette pan.

2. Meanwhile, beat together the eggs and milk. Season well. Once the butter is frothy, tip the mixture into the pan, swirling to coat the pan evenly.

## Omelette With Crispy Bacon/cont.

3. As the mixture begins to set, gradually push the runny edges of the omelette into the centre of the pan using a spatula.

4. Continue to cook for a further 3-4 minutes or until almost set, then use a spatula to push the omelette onto a plate, folding it as you go. Serve immediately.

5. Grill the bacon for 5 minutes until crispy or as desired.

## Fruity Porridge

Preparation time: 10 minutes
Serves 1-2

### Ingredients

500ml (16fl oz) milk
2.5 tablespoons porridge oats
1 banana
100g (4oz) fresh raspberries/blueberries
demerara sugar to taste

### Preparation

1. Pour milk into pan and add your oats, keep stirring until it begins to thicken.

2. Chop banana and add to porridge whilst still stirring. Add sugar to demerara taste.

3. Pour into bowl and sprinkle your choice of fresh berries.

## Breakfast Muffins

Preparation time: 35 minutes
Makes: 12 muffins

Breakfast

## Ingredients

300g (11oz) plain wholemeal flour
50g (2oz) rolled porridge oats, plus extra for decoration
3 heaped teaspoons baking powder
1/2 teaspoon mixed spice
1/2 teaspoon ground cinnamon
100g (4oz) raisins
100g (4oz) dried apricots, chopped
50g (2oz) pecans, chopped
50g (2oz) caster sugar
100ml (3.5fl oz) sunflower oil
150ml (5fl oz) natural yogurt
150ml (5fl oz) milk
1 medium egg, beaten
2 medium bananas, mashed
1 teaspoon vanilla extract
2 small apples, grated
1 medium carrot, coarsely grated

## To Decorate

sunflower and pumpkin seeds

## Preparation

1. Preheat oven to 190°C (375°F / Gas Mark 5). Lightly oil a non-stick muffin pan with 12 large cups (or two six-cup pans).

2. Combine the first nine ingredients (the dry ingredients) in a large bowl and set aside.

3. In a separate bowl, mix the remaining ingredients (wet) well. Mix both lots of ingredients together and stir until just combined. Spoon into the prepared muffin pans.

## *Breakfast Muffins/cont.*

4. Sprinkle with oats, sunflower and pumpkin seeds, and bake for 20 minutes or until a skewer inserted into the middle comes out clean. Leave in the tin for a further 5 minutes, then cool on a rack. Eat when still warm.

### Useful Tip

You can prepare the dry and wet ingredients the night before. Combine the two in the morning and you'll have a fresh-baked breakfast.

## *English Muffins*

Preparation time: 2 hours
Makes 12

### Ingredients

450g (16oz) strong plain flour
1 teaspoon salt
55ml (2fl oz) water
225ml (8fl oz) milk
1 teaspoon caster sugar
2 teaspoons dried yeast
50g (2oz) lard

You will also need a thick, solid-based frying pan or a girdle.

### Preparation

1. Pour the milk and water into a small saucepan and heat until hot enough that you can dip your finger in without scalding it.

2. Pour it into a jug, add the sugar and dried yeast, mix it with a fork and leave it for about 10 minutes to get a very frothy head.

3. Sift the flour and salt into a large mixing bowl, making a well in the centre, then pour in the frothy yeast mixture and mix it to a soft dough - it should leave the bowl cleanly but if it seems a bit sticky add a spot more flour. On the other hand, if it seems a little dry add just a dash of water.

seems a little dry add just a dash of water.

4. Transfer the dough to a flat surface and knead it for about 10 minutes by which time it should be very smooth and elastic. The dough can go back into the bowl now. Place the bowl inside a large polythene bag and leave it in a warm place until the dough has doubled in size. This will take about 45 minutes or longer, depending on the temperature.

5. When the dough has risen, lightly flour the work surface, then tip the dough out and roll it out to about 10mm (0.5inch) thick. Then, using a 7.5cm (3inch) plain cutter, cut out 12 rounds, re-rolling the dough a couple of times again if it starts to get puffy. Mix the scraps and re-roll as well to use it all up.

6. Place the muffins on an ungreased, lightly floured baking sheet, sprinkling them with a little more flour, then leave them to puff up again for about 25-35 minutes in a warm place.

7. When they are ready to be cooked, grease a thick-based frying pan or griddle with a small amount of lard, then heat the pan over a medium heat, add some muffins and cook them for about 7 minutes on each side, turning the heat down to low as soon as they go in. You'll need to do this in 3 or 4 batches but they can be made well in advance.

8. To serve, break them just a little around their waists without opening them, then toast them lightly on both sides. Serve with lots of butter and your favourite jam or marmalade. You can store them in an airtight tin for about two days before toasting.

## Kedgeree

Preparation time: 45 minutes
Serves 6

### Ingredients

2 large eggs
680g (24oz) smoked haddock fillets
2 fresh bay leaves
170g (6oz) long grain or basmati rice
sea salt
110g (4oz) butter
1 medium onion or 1 bunch of spring onions, finely chopped
1 clove of garlic, peeled & finely chopped
2 heaped tablespoons curry powder
1 tablespoon mustard seeds
2 tomatoes, deseeded & chopped
juice of 2 lemons
2 good handfuls of fresh coriander, leaves picked & chopped
1 fresh red chilli, finely chopped
small pot of natural yoghurt

### Preparation

1. Boil the eggs for 10 minutes, then cool under cold running water.

2. Put the fish and bay leaves in a shallow pan with enough water to cover. Bring to the boil, cover and simmer for about 5 minutes until cooked through. Remove from pan and leave to cool.

3. Remove the skin from fish, flake into chunks and set aside.

4. Cook the rice in salted water for about 10 minutes and drain. Refresh in cold water, drain again, and leave in the fridge until needed.

5. Melt the butter in a pan over a low heat and add the onion and garlic. Soften for about 5 minutes, then add the curry powder and mustard seeds.

6. Cook for a further few minutes, then add the chopped tomatoes and lemon juice.

7. Quarter the eggs. Add the fish and rice to a pan and gently heat through. Add the eggs, most of the coriander and the chilli and stir gently.

8. Place in a warm serving dish. Mix the rest of the coriander into the yoghurt and serve with the kedgeree.

## *Eggs Benedict*
Preparation time: 30 minutes
Serves 4

### Ingredients
4 egg yolks
50ml (2fl oz) lemon juice
15g (1/2oz) ground white pepper
1 teaspoon Worcestershire sauce
1 tablespoon water
225g (8oz) butter, melted
8 eggs
sprinkle of salt
1 teaspoon white vinegar
8 rashers bacon
4 English muffins, split
30g (1oz) butter, softened

### Preparation
1. To make the Hollandaise sauce, fill the bottom of a double boiler part-way with water. Make sure that water does not touch the top pan. Bring water to a gentle simmer. In the top of the double boiler, whisk together egg yolks, lemon juice, white pepper, Worcestershire sauce and 1 tablespoon water.

2. Add the melted butter to egg yolk mixture 1 or 2 tablespoons at a time while whisking yolks constantly. If the Hollandaise begins to get too thick, add

## *Eggs Benedict/cont.*

a teaspoon or two of hot water. Continue whisking until all of the butter has been added. Whisk in salt, then remove from heat. Place a lid on pan to keep sauce warm.

3. Preheat oven on grill setting.

4. To poach the eggs, fill a large saucepan with 8cm (3inches) of water. Bring water to a gentle simmer, then add vinegar. Carefully break eggs into simmering water, and allow to cook for 2.5 to 3 minutes. Yolks should still be soft in centre.

5. Remove eggs from water with a slotted spoon and set on a warm plate.

6. While eggs are poaching, cook the bacon in a pan over a medium-high heat and toast the English muffins on a baking sheet under the grill or in the toaster.

7. Spread toasted muffins with softened butter, and top each one with a slice of bacon, followed by one poached egg. Place 2 muffins on each plate and drizzle with hollandaise sauce. Sprinkle with chopped chives and serve immediately.

# Comfort Food

## Cottage Pie
Preparation time: 30 minutes
Cooking time: 2-2.5 hours
Serves 6-8

### Ingredients
### For the mince
50ml (2fl oz) olive oil
650g (1lb 7oz) minced beef
3-4 shallots, finely chopped
4 sprigs fresh thyme
30g (1oz) tomato purée
15g (3/4oz) plain flour
150ml (5fl oz) red wine
200ml (7fl oz) beef stock
salt & freshly ground black pepper
Worcestershire sauce, to taste

### For the mash
900g (2lb) King Edward potatoes, peeled & chopped
115g (4oz) butter
125ml (4.5fl oz) double cream
salt & freshly ground black pepper

### Preparation
1. Heat a large frying pan until smoking, add half of the olive oil and fry the minced beef, in batches, for 4-5 minutes, or until browned all over.

2. Heat a separate pan until smoking, add the remaining olive oil and fry the shallots and thyme for 2-3 minutes, or until just softened. Stir in the tomato purée and flour and cook for a further minute, then add the cooked beef.

3. Deglaze the frying pan used to cook the beef with the red wine,

## Cottage Pie/cont.

scraping at any caramelised bits with a wooden spoon. Cook for 3-4 minutes, or until the wine has reduced by half, then pour the wine into the pan with the beef.

4. Add the stock to the pan and leave to simmer for 1-2 hours, or until the beef is tender and the mixture is thickened. Season to taste with salt, freshly ground black pepper and a few dashes of Worcestershire sauce. Keep warm over a very low heat.

5. Preheat the grill to high.

6. For the mash, place the potatoes into a pan of salted water and bring to the boil. Reduce the heat and simmer for 12-15 minutes, until the potatoes are tender.

7. Drain and return the potatoes to the pan, then place over the heat for about one minute to get rid of any excess moisture. Mash well with a potato masher or ricer, then add the butter and milk, beating to form a smooth mash. Season, to taste, with salt and freshly ground black pepper. Spoon the mash into a piping bag.

8. To serve, place the mince mixture into a baking dish and pipe the mash over the top. Place under the grill for 8-10 minutes, or until the top is golden brown. Serve spooned onto serving plates.

## Vegetable Soup

Preparation time: 40 minutes
Serves 4

### Ingredients

25g (1oz) unsalted butter
1 red onion, chopped
2 garlic cloves, finely chopped
175g (6oz) turnip, peeled and cut into 1cm (1/2inch) cubes
175g (6oz) sweet potato, peeled & cut into 1cm (1/2inch) cubes
175g (6oz) pumpkin, peeled & cut into 1cm cubes (1/2inch)
1 teaspoon coriander seeds, ground
1 teaspoon ground ginger

15g (3/4oz) spring onions, chopped
salt & freshly ground black pepper
1 litre (32fl oz) vegetable stock
2 tablespoons flaked almonds, toasted
1 fresh chilli, de-seeded & chopped
1 teaspoon caster sugar
2 tablespoons coconut milk

## Preparation

1. Melt the butter in a large non-stick saucepan. Add the onion and garlic and fry for 6-8 minutes over a medium heat.

2. Add the cubed vegetables and fry for 3-4 minutes.

3. Add the ground coriander, ground ginger, spring onions and salt and freshly ground black pepper, to taste. Fry over a low heat for about 5 minutes, stirring frequently.

4. Add the vegetable stock, flaked almonds, chopped chilli and sugar and stir well to mix. Cover and simmer gently for 10-15 minutes, until the vegetables are just tender.

5. Pour the coconut milk into the soup mix and stir.

## Lamb Stew With Dumplings

Preparation time: 2 hours
Serves 6-8

### Ingredients
### For the stew

750g (27oz) lamb neck fillet, cut into 2.5cm (1inch) cubes
salt & freshly ground black pepper
25g (1oz) plain flour
1 tablespoon olive oil
50g (2oz) butter
12 baby onions, peeled
2 carrots, chopped
1 swede, chopped
50ml (2fl oz) white wine
1250ml (40fl oz) lamb stock
4 bay leaves
2 sprigs rosemary
3 tablespoons chopped fresh flatleaf parsley

### For the dumplings

125g (5oz) plain flour, plus extra for dusting
65g (2.5oz) suet
1/2 teaspoon baking powder
pinch salt
3-5 tablespoons cold water
500ml (16fl oz) lamb stock

### Preparation

1. Preheat the oven to 140°C (275°F / Gas Mark 1).

2. For the stew, season the lamb with salt and freshly ground black pepper and dust with the flour.

3. Heat the olive oil with the butter in a heavy-based casserole dish, add the lamb

Comfort Food

and fry for 2-3 minutes on each side, or until golden-brown all over. Transfer the lamb onto a plate and set aside.

4. Lower the heat and add the onions, carrots and swede to the pan and fry for 6-7 minutes, or until they begin to caramelise.

5. Pour in the wine and cook until the liquid has reduced by half, then add the lamb pieces and the lamb stock. Bring to a simmer, then add the bay leaves and rosemary and cover with a lid.

6. Place into the oven to cook for one hour, or until the lamb is soft and tender.

7. For the dumplings, mix together the flour, suet, baking powder and a pinch of salt in a bowl, then mix in enough water to form a sticky dough.

8. With floured hands, break pieces off the dough and roll into 12 little balls. Transfer the dumplings onto a plate and place into the fridge to chill for 10-15 minutes.

9. Pour the lamb stock into a pan and bring to a simmer, then add the dumplings and cook for 6-8 minutes, or until cooked through. Using a slotted spoon, transfer the dumplings onto a warm dish and discard the cooking stock.

10. To serve, stir the dumplings and parsley into the lamb casserole.

15

## *Lamb Hotpot*

Preparation time: 10 minutes
Cooking time: 2 hours 45 minutes
Serves 6-8

## Ingredients

2 large red onions, chopped
3 medium carrots, chopped
1 turnip, chopped
900g (2lb) best end of neck of lamb chops, or cubed leg of lamb
1 bay leaf
salt & freshly ground black pepper
8 x 2.5cm (1inch) thick slices black pudding
900g (2lb) potatoes, sliced into 5mm (1/4inch) thick slices
570ml (19fl oz) hot lamb stock
55g (2oz) butter, melted

## Preparation

1. Preheat the oven to 180°C (350°F / Gas Mark 4).

2. Place the red onions, carrots and turnips into a heavy-based casserole dish with a lid. Add the lamb and bay leaf and season with salt and freshly ground black pepper.

3. Cover the lamb and vegetables with the black pudding slices followed by a layer of potato slices, overlapping the slices to completely cover the lamb, vegetables and black pudding.

4. Add the hot stock to the casserole and brush the potatoes with melted butter.

5. Cover the casserole and place in the oven to cook for about two hours. After two hours remove the lid and cook for another 30-45 minutes, until the potatoes are crisp and golden-brown.

6. Take the casserole dish to the table and serve.

Comfort Food

## *Fish Pie*

Preparation time: 60 minutes
Serves 4-6

### Ingredients

sea salt & freshly ground black pepper
1kg (36oz) potatoes
1 carrot
2 sticks of celery
150g (5oz) Cheddar cheese
1 lemon
1/2 fresh red chilli
4 sprigs of fresh flat-leaf parsley
300g (11oz) salmon fillets, skin off & bones removed
300g (11oz) undyed smoked haddock fillets, skin off & bones removed
125g (4.5oz) king prawns, raw, peeled
olive oil

### Preparation

1. Boil the potatoes ready to mash. Meanwhile, get yourself a deep baking tray or earthenware dish and stand a box grater in it.

2. Peel the carrot. Grate the celery, carrot and Cheddar on the coarse side of the grater.

3. Use the fine side of the grater to grate the zest from the lemon.

4. Finely grate or chop your chilli.

5. Finely chop the parsley leaves and stalks and add these to the tray. Cut the salmon and smoked haddock into bite-size chunks and add to the tray with the prawns.

6. Squeeze over the juice from the zested lemon (no pips please!), drizzle with olive oil and add a good pinch of salt and pepper.

## *Fish Pie/cont.*

7. Mix everything together really well.

8. By now your potatoes should be cooked, so drain them in a colander and return them to the pan.

9. Drizzle with a couple of good lugs of olive oil and add a pinch of salt and pepper.

10. Mash until nice and smooth, then spread evenly over the top of the fish and grated vegetables.

11. Place in the preheated oven for around 40 minutes, or until cooked through, crispy and golden on top.

## *Cornish Pasty*

Preparation time: 60 minutes
Serves 6

### Ingredients

Pastry for double crust 9inch pie
250ml (8fl oz) cooked cubed beef
1 small potato, peeled & diced
1 small carrot, peeled & thinly sliced
1 medium onion, finely chopped
50ml (2fl oz) gravy
1 tablespoon steak sauce
1/4 teaspoon salt
1/4 teaspoon pepper

### Preparation

1. Mix all filling ingredients. Roll out 6-6.5inch pastry circles. Divide filling among circles.

2. For each pastry, bring up two sides above filling and pinch together, crimping to make a wavy edge. Brush with egg or milk.

# Comfort Food

3. Place on a lightly greased baking tray.

4. Bake at 220°C (425°F / Gas Mark 7) for 15 minutes, reducing heat to 180°C (350°F / Gas Mark 4) for 30 minutes.

5. Can be served hot or cold.

## Cheese & Potato Bake

Preparation time: 60 minutes
Serves 4-6

### Ingredients

900g (32oz) potatoes
450g (16oz) leeks
450g (16oz) courgette
300ml (10fl oz) vegetable stock
225g (8oz) button mushrooms
1 large onion
160g (6oz) Cheddar cheese, grated
50g (2oz) butter
25g (1oz) plain flour
3 tablespoons milk
2 teaspoons paprika

### Preparation

1. Cut the potato into cubes, slice the leeks, onion and courgettes.

2. Boil the potatoes in salted water for 15-20 minutes or until tender.

3. Drain and mash with the milk, half the cheese and half the butter.

4. Heat the remaining butter in a large pan and fry the leeks and onion until softened, approximately 4-5 minutes.

## Cheese & Potato Bake/cont.

5. Add the courgettes, mushrooms and paprika and fry for 2 more minutes.

6. Sprinkle in the flour, then slowly add the stock and bring to the boil, stirring continuously. Cover and allow to simmer for 5 minutes.

7. Pre-heat oven to 200°C (400°F / Gas Mark 6)

8. Spoon the vegetable mixture into an ovenproof dish and cover with the potato mixture, sprinkling with the remaining cheese.

9. Bake for 20-25 minutes or until the top is crisp and golden brown.

## Welsh Rarebit

Preparation time: 10 minutes
Serves 2

### Ingredients
225g (8oz) Cheddar/Cheshire Cheese
2 Slices of toast
1/2 onion
2 tablespoons beer
1 teaspoon English mustard

### Preparation
1. Preheat the oven on grill setting.

2. Grate the cheese and onion then mix with beer and mustard.

3. Place half of the mixture on each slice of toast.

4. Grill until the cheese is melted and golden brown.

5. Add sliced tomato or grilled bacon as an alternative.

# Cauliflower Cheese

Preparation time: 45 minutes
Serves 4

## Ingredients

1 large cauliflower
300ml (10fl oz) milk
110g (4oz) cheddar cheese
3 tablespoons plain flour
50g (2oz) butter
25g (1oz) fresh breadcrumbs
1/2 teaspoon mustard
nutmeg
salt & black pepper

## Preparation

1. Trim the cauliflower and boil in salted water for 10-15 minutes or until just tender.

2. Drain and place in a flameproof dish.

3. Add the milk, flour and butter to a saucepan.

4. Heat, stirring continuously until the sauce thickens, boils and is smooth. Allow to simmer for a further 2 minutes.

5. Add three-quarters of the grated cheese, mustard, a pinch of nutmeg and seasoning. Cook for a further minute stirring well.

6. Pour the sauce over the cauliflower.

7. Mix the remaining cheese and breadcrumbs together, sprinkle over the top.

8. Place under a hot grill until golden brown. Serve immediately.

# *Luxury Toad in the Hole*

Preparation time: 60 minutes
Serves 4

## Ingredients

### For the Yorkshire pudding

250ml (8fl oz) milk
1 egg, well-beaten
100g (4oz) sifted plain flour
1/4 teaspoon salt

### For the Filling

4 pork sausages, quartered
4 rashers of bacon, diced
1/2 onion, chopped
100g (4oz) Cheddar cheese, diced
25g (1oz) butter to grease the baking dish (non-stick)

## Preparation

1. Preheat the oven to 200°C (400°F / Gas Mark 6).

2. Grease a medium size non-stick baking dish with the butter.

3. Place the flour with the salt in a bowl, drop the egg in the centre and start to stir in with a fork. Gradually add the milk a little at a time to incorporate all the flour into a batter with no lumps. Beat with the fork, a balloon whisk or rotary whisk for a few minutes (note - you can pop the flour, salt, egg and milk in a blender for a minute or two instead).

4. Pour the batter into the baking dish and roughly arrange the sausages, bacon, onion and cheese so they are well spread out to assist serving.

5. Cook for 30 to 40 minutes on the top shelf of the oven until the batter has risen and golden brown.

6. Can be served hot or cold.

## Bubble & Squeak

Preparation time: 60 minutes
Serves 4-6

### Ingredients

450g (16oz) potatoes, unpeeled
salt & pepper
70g (2.5oz) butter
250g (8oz) cabbage, shredded
3 tablespoons water
3-4 tablespoons sunflower oil
1 onion, chopped

### Preparation

1. Cook the potatoes for 25 minutes in a pan of lightly salted boiling water, then drain, peel and dice.

2. Place them in a bowl with 55g (2oz) of the butter and mash until smooth. Season to taste with salt and pepper.

3. Meanwhile, place the cabbage, water and remaining butter in a large heavy based saucepan and cover. Cook gently for 10 minutes, or until tender. Mix the cabbage and mashed potato together and season with more salt and pepper.

4. Heat half the oil in a frying pan. Add the onion and cook, stirring occasionally until softened. Add the potato and cabbage mixture and press down with the back of a wooden spoon to make a flat, even cake.

5. Cook over a medium heat for 15 minutes until golden brown on the underside and place on a large plate. Add the remaining oil and cook again on the other side for 10 minutes.

6. Transfer to a plate, cut into wedges and serve.

## Chilli Con Carne

Preparation time: 60 minutes
Serves 4-6

### Ingredients

1 tablespoon oil
1 large onion
1 red pepper
2 garlic cloves, peeled
1 heaped teaspoon hot chilli powder
1 teaspoon paprika
1 teaspoon ground cumin
500g (18oz) lean minced beef
1 beef stock cube
400g (14oz) can of chopped tomatoes
1/2 teaspoon dried marjoram
1 teaspoon sugar
2 tablespoons tomato purée
400g (14oz) can of red kidney beans
soured cream & plain boiled long grain rice, to serve

### Preparation

1. Dice the onion into small cubes, about 5mm (1/4inch) square.

2. Put your pan on a medium heat. Add the oil and leave it for 1-2 minutes until hot. Add the onions and cook, stirring fairly frequently, for about 5 minutes, or until the onions are soft, squidgy and slightly translucent.

3. Tip in the garlic, red pepper, chilli, paprika and cumin. Give it a good stir, then leave it to cook for another 5 minutes, stirring occasionally.

Comfort Food

4. Brown the mince. Turn the heat up a bit, add the meat to the pan and break it up with your spoon or spatula. The mix should sizzle a bit when you add the mince.

5. Keep stirring and prodding for at least 5 minutes, until all the mince is in uniform, mince-sized lumps and there are no more pink bits. Make sure you keep the heat hot enough for the meat to fry and become brown, rather than just stew.

6. To make the sauce, crumble your stock cube into 300ml (11oz) of hot water. Pour this into the pan with the mince mixture. Open the can of chopped tomatoes and add these as well.

7. Tip in the marjoram and the sugar, and add a good shake of salt and pepper. Squirt in about 2 tablespoons of tomato purée and stir the sauce well.

8. Simmer it gently. Bring the whole thing to the boil, give it a good stir and put a lid on the pan. Turn down the heat until it is gently bubbling and leave it for 20 minutes. You should check on the pan occasionally to stir it and make sure the sauce doesn't stick to the bottom of the pan or isn't drying out. If it is, add a couple of tablespoons of water and make sure that the heat really is low enough.

9. After simmering gently, the saucy mince mixture should look thick, moist and juicy.

10. Drain and rinse the beans in a sieve and stir them into the chilli pot. Bring to the boil again, and gently bubble without the lid for another 10 minutes, adding a little more water if it looks too dry.

11. Season to taste.

12. Turn off the heat and leave your chilli to stand for 10 minutes before serving.

## *Beef & Ale Pie*
Preparation time: 30-60 minutes
Cooking time: 2 hours
Serves 4-6

## *Beef & Ale Pie/cont.*

### Ingredients

900g (32oz) Scotch beef stewing steak
vegetable oil
1 medium onion, peeled & diced
1 tablespoon plain flour
1 tablespoon Worcestershire sauce
1 handful fresh thyme, marjoram & chopped parsley
1 teaspoon English mustard
1 bay leaf
salt & cracked black peppercorns
150ml (5fl oz) beef stock
125ml (4.5fl oz) ale
225g (9oz) mushrooms
450g (16oz) puff pastry

### Preparation

1. Cut the beef into cubes about 2.5cm (1inch) square.

2. Heat oil in a saucepan and fry onion, without colouring.

3. Add beef, making sure the meat is at room temperature first, and cook until medium brown.

4. Stir in the flour and cook until dark brown (about 1 minute).

5. Add Worcestershire sauce, thyme, marjoram, mustard, bay leaf and seasoning.

6. Slowly add beef stock and ale then bring to the boil.

7. Add mushrooms and simmer gently until beef is almost tender for approximately 90 minutes.

8. Preheat oven to 200°C (400°F / Gas Mark 6).

9. Remove meat from heat, skim off any fat, adjust seasoning and add fresh chopped parsley.

10. Place in pie dish or individual dishes. Cover pie dish (or dishes) with the pastry and trim edges.

11. Bake for 20-25 minutes or until pastry is well-risen and golden brown.

## *Chicken Chasseur*

Preparation time: 1.5-2 hours
Serves 4-6

### Ingredients

1 teaspoon olive oil
25g (1oz) butter
4 chicken legs
1 onion, chopped
2 garlic cloves, crushed
200g (7oz) pack small button or chestnut mushrooms
225ml (7.5fl oz) red wine
2 tablespoons tomato purée
2 thyme sprigs
500ml (16fl oz) chicken stock

### Preparation

1. Heat the oil and half the butter in a large lidded casserole. Season the chicken, then fry for about 5 minutes on each side until golden brown. Remove and set aside.

2. Melt the rest of the butter in the pan. Add the onion, then fry for about 5 minutes until soft. Add garlic, cook for about 1 minute, add the mushrooms, cook for 2 minutes, then add the wine. Stir in the tomato purée, let the liquid bubble and reduce for about 5 minutes, then stir in the thyme and pour over the stock. Slip the chicken back into the pan, then cover and simmer on a low heat for about 1 hour until the chicken is very tender.

## Chicken Chasseur/cont.

3. Remove the chicken from the pan and keep warm. Rapidly boil down the sauce for 10 minutes or so until it is syrupy and the flavour has concentrated. Put the chicken legs back into the sauce and serve.

## Beef Stroganoff

Preparation time: 30 minutes
Serves 4

### Ingredients

450g (16oz) top sirloin, cut into finger size strips
1 onion, finely chopped
50g (2oz) butter
225g (8oz) mushrooms, coarsely chopped
2 cloves garlic, finely chopped
1 tablespoon tomato purée
1 cup of double cream
150ml (5fl oz) of sherry or brandy
Handful chopped parsley
Pinch of salt & pepper

### Preparation

1. Place butter, garlic and onions in pan and gently cook for 2 minutes. Place the sirloin strips and mushrooms in the same pan and gently stir all ingredients for 5 minutes.

2. Place tomato purée, cream, sherry/brandy, salt and pepper into the meat mixture and simmer for 15 minutes, stirring occassionaly.

3. Serve with boiled rice and sprinkle with the chopped parsley.

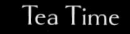

# Tea Time

## Hot Cross Buns

Preparation time: 2 hours
Makes 24

### Ingredients

250ml (8fl oz) milk
2 tablespoons yeast
125g (4.5oz) sugar
2 teaspoons salt
100g (4oz) butter, melted & cooled
1.5 teaspoons cinnamon
1/2 teaspoon nutmeg
4 eggs
1kg (36oz) flour
375g (13oz) currants or raisins
1 egg white

### For the Glaze

375g (13oz) confectioner's sugar
1.5 teaspoons finely chopped lemon zest
1/2 teaspoon lemon extract
1-2 tablespoons milk

### Preparation

1. In a small saucepan, heat milk until it starts to simmer. Pour warm milk in a bowl and sprinkle yeast over. Mix to dissolve and allow to sit for 5 minutes.

2. Stirring constantly, add sugar, salt, butter, cinnamon, nutmeg and eggs. Gradually mix in flour, dough will be wet and sticky.

3. Continue kneading until smooth, about 5 minutes. Cover bowl with plastic wrap and let the dough "rest" for 30-45 minutes.

## *Hot Cross Buns/cont.*

4. Knead again until smooth and elastic, for about 3 more minutes. Add currants or raisins and knead until well mixed. At this point, dough will still be fairly wet and sticky.

5. Shape dough in a ball, place in a buttered dish, cover with plastic wrap and allow to rise overnight in the refrigerator. Excess moisture will be absorbed by the morning. Let dough sit at room temperature for 30 minutes.

6. Line a large baking pan or pans with parchment paper. Divide dough into 24 equal pieces.

7. Shape each portion into a ball and place on baking sheet, about 15mm (1/2inch) inch apart. Cover with a clean kitchen towel and allow to rise in a warm, draft-free place until doubled in size, about 90 minutes.

8. In the meantime, preheat oven to 200°C (400°F / Gas Mark 6).

9. When buns have risen, take a sharp or serrated knife and carefully slash buns with a cross. Brush them with egg white and place in oven.

10. Bake for 10 minutes, then reduce heat to 180°C (350°F / Gas Mark 4), then bake until golden brown, about 15 minutes more. Transfer to a wire rack.

11. Whisk together glaze ingredients, and spoon over buns in a cross pattern.

Serve warm.

**Tea Time**

## *Victoria Sponge With Jam*

Preparation time: 30 minutes
Serves 8

### Ingredients
### For the Cake

knob of butter, melted
225g (8oz) butter, softened
225g (8oz) caster sugar
4 large free-range eggs
225g (8oz) self-raising flour, sifted

### For the Filling

6 tablespoons good-quality strawberry jam
300ml (10fl oz) double cream, lightly whipped

### To Serve

icing sugar, for dusting

### Preparation

1. Preheat the oven to 180°C (350°F / Gas Mark 4).

2. Gently heat the knob of butter in a pan and brush two 15cm (6inch) cake tins with the melted butter. Line the bottom of the two cake tins with a circle of greaseproof paper.

3. In a large bowl, cream together the butter and sugar until pale and creamy, using an electric whisk or a wooden spoon. Beat well to get lots of air into the mixture (this should take a couple of minutes).

4. Beat in the eggs one at a time. Add a tablespoon of flour if the mixture curdles.

5. Fold in the flour using a large metal spoon. Be careful not to over-mix it.

6. Pour the mixture equally between the two cake tins and level off the top

## *Victoria Sponge With Jam/cont.*

with a spatula. Make a slight dip in the centre with the tip of the spatula if you don't want them to be pointed in the middle.

7. Place in the oven and bake for about 20 minutes, or until the cakes spring back when pressed gently with a finger and are pale golden in colour.

8. Remove from the oven and take them out of the tins after about 5-10 minutes. Place them on a wire rack to cool completely (for about half an hour).

9. Spread the sponge with the jam and the whipped cream, then carefully sandwich together.

10. Dust with icing sugar and serve.


## *Rock Cakes*
Preparation time: 20-30 minutes
Makes 6-10

### Ingredients
450g (16oz) caster sugar
225g (8oz) flour
6 eggs
handful of currants

### Preparation
1. Beat the eggs well until very light, add the sugar.

2. When well mixed, sift in the flour gradually and add the currants. Mix together well.

3. Put the dough, with a fork, on the baking trays, making it look as rough as possible.

4. Bake the cakes in a moderate oven for 20 to 30 minutes.

5. Allow to cool before serving. Store them away in a tin, in a cool, dry place.

## *Fruit Scones*

Preparation time: 30 minutes
Makes 12

### Ingredients

500g (18oz) self-raising flour
12g (1/2oz) baking powder
A pinch salt
125g (4oz) butter
125g (4oz) caster sugar
250ml (8fl oz) milk or water
150g (5oz) sultanas

### Preparation

1. Sieve the flour, baking powder and salt into a bowl.

2. Rub in the butter until you have a sandy texture. Make a well in the centre.

3. Dissolve the sugar in the liquid and add to the well in the mixture.

4. Gradually incorporate the flour with the sugary liquid and mix.

5. Roll out 2 rounds of the mixture 1cm (1/2inch) thick and place on a greased baking sheet.

6. Cut across halfway through the rounds with a large knife.

7. Milk-wash and bake at 200°C (400°F / Gas Mark 6) for 15-20 minutes.

## Gingerbread Man

Preparation time: 30 minutes
Makes 12-14

### Ingredients
125g (4.5oz) plain wholemeal flour
1/2 teaspoon each bicarbonate of soda & ground cinnamon
1 teaspoon ground ginger
25g (1oz) margarine
50g (2oz) muscovado sugar
1 tablespoon clear honey
1 teaspoon orange juice
50g (2oz) curd cheese
a little milk to mix

### Preparation

1. Preheat the oven to 160°C (325°F / Gas Mark 3). Place the flour in a mixing bowl and sift in the soda and spices.

2. Place the margarine, sugar and honey in a pan and heat gently, stirring until melted. Cool, then pour onto the flour with the orange juice and mix to form a firm dough.

3. Turn onto a floured surface and roll out to about 5mm (1/6inch) thick. Using a gingerbread man cutter, cut out 12-14 men and place on greased baking sheets.

4. Bake for 10-15 minutes until firm. Cool on a wire rack.

5. Mix the curd cheese with a little milk to give a smooth consistency. Spoon into a greaseproof paper piping bag fitted with a writing nozzle and pipe eyes, nose, mouth and button on each man.

> Tea Time

## *Jam Roly Poly*

Preparation time: 40 minutes
Serves 4-6

### Ingredients

115g (4oz) butter, cut into cubes, plus extra for greasing
115g (4oz) caster sugar, plus extra for sprinkling
3 free-range eggs
175g (6oz) self-raising flour
1/2 teaspoon cornflour
4 tablespoons raspberry jam
double cream, to serve

### Preparation

1. Preheat the oven to 180°C (350°F / Gas Mark 4).

2. Place the butter and sugar into a food processor and pulse until the mixture resembles breadcrumbs.

3. Crack in the eggs and blend until combined.

4. Add the flour and cornflour and blend until the mixture forms a smooth batter.

5. Grease and flour a 20x30cm (8x12inch) Swiss roll tin and shake out the excess flour. Pour the batter into the prepared tin and smooth to the edges using a spatula.

6. Transfer to the oven and bake for 10-12 minutes, or until lightly golden brown and springy to the touch.

7. Place a sheet of baking paper on a work surface and sprinkle with sugar. Carefully turn the cake out onto the sugared paper, cover with a clean damp tea towel and leave to cool.

8. Heat the jam in a small pan for 2-3 minutes, then pass through a sieve into

## *Jam Roly Poly/cont.*
a bowl to remove the seeds.

9. Remove the damp tea towel from the cake and spread the jam over the unsugared side. Roll the cake up in the shape of a sausage using the paper underneath to help you.

10. To serve, cut the Swiss roll into four large slices and place onto serving plates, then drizzle with double cream.


## *Lemon Drizzle Cake*
Preparation time: 45-60 minutes
Serves 6-8

### Ingredients

200g (7oz) butter, well softened, plus extra
200g (7oz) golden caster sugar
4 large eggs
100g (4oz) fine polenta or fine cornmeal
140g (5oz) self-raising flour
zest of 3 lemons

### For The Swirl & Drizzle

4 tablespoons lemon curd
5 tablespoons golden or white caster sugar
zest & juice of 1 lemon

### Preparation

1. Heat oven to 180°C (350°F / Gas Mark 4) and make sure there's a shelf ready in the middle of the oven.

2. Butter a rectangular baking tray or small roasting tin, about 20x30cm (8x12inch).

3. Cut out a sheet of baking paper a bit larger than the tin, then push it in and

Tea Time

smooth it out with your hands so it sticks to the butter. Snip into the corners with a pair of scissors to get the paper to lie neatly.

4. Put all the cake ingredients and a pinch of salt into a large bowl, then use electric beaters to beat until creamy and smooth. Scoop into the tin, then level the top.

5. Spoon the lemon curd over the batter in thick stripes. Use the handle of the spoon to swirl the curd into the cake - not too much or you won't see the swirls once it's cooked.

6. Bake for about 35 minutes or until golden and risen. It should have shrunk away from the sides of the tin ever so slightly and feel springy. Don't open the oven before 30 minutes cooking is up.

7. Leave the cake in the tin for 10 minutes or until just cool enough to handle. Carefully lift out of the tin and put it onto a cooling rack, sat over a tray or something similar to catch drips of drizzle.

8. To make the drizzle, mix 4 tablespoons sugar and the lemon juice together and spoon over the cake. Toss the lemon zest with the final one tablespoon of sugar and scatter over the top.

9. Let the cake cool completely, then lift onto a board, peel away the sides of the baking paper and cut the cake into fingers. Store in an airtight tin for up to 3 days.

## *Chocolate Cake*

Preparation time: 2 hours
Serves 6-8

### Ingredients

200g (7oz) good quality dark chocolate, about 60% cocoa solids
200g (7oz) butter, cut in pieces
1 tablespoon instant coffee granules
85g (4oz) self-raising flour

## *Chocolate Cake/cont.*

85g (4oz) plain flour
1/4 teaspoon bicarbonate of soda
200g (7oz) light muscovado sugar
200g (7oz) golden caster sugar
25g (1oz) cocoa powder
3 medium eggs
75ml (2.5fl oz) buttermilk
grated chocolate or curls, to decorate

## For The Ganache

200g (7oz) good-quality dark chocolate, as above
300ml (10fl oz) double cream
2 tablespoons golden caster sugar

## Preparation

1. Preheat the oven to fan 160°C (325°F / Gas Mark 3) .

2. Butter a 20cm (8inch) round cake tin (7.5cm (3inch) deep) and line the base. Break the chocolate into pieces into a medium, heavy-based pan.

3. Tip in the butter, then mix the coffee granules into 125ml (4fl oz) cold water and pour into the pan. Warm through over a low heat just until everything is melted - don't overheat.

4. While the chocolate is melting, mix the two flours, bicarbonate of soda, sugars and cocoa in a big bowl, mixing with your hands to get rid of any lumps. Beat the eggs in a bowl and stir in the buttermilk.

5. Pour the melted chocolate mixture and the egg mixture into the flour mixture, stirring until everything is well blended and you have a smooth, quite runny consistency.

6. Pour this into the tin and bake for 1 hour 25 minutes-1 hour 30 minutes. If you push a skewer in the centre it should come out clean and the top should feel firm.

Tea Time

7. Leave to cool in the tin (don't worry if it dips slightly), then turn out onto a wire rack to cool completely.

8. When the cake is cold, cut it horizontally into three.

9. To make the ganache, chop the chocolate into small pieces and tip into a bowl. Pour the cream into a pan, add the sugar, and heat until it is about to boil.

10. Take off the heat and pour it over the chocolate. Stir until the chocolate has melted and the mixture is smooth.

11. Sandwich the layers together with just a little of the ganache. Pour the rest over the cake letting it fall down the sides and smoothing to cover with a palette knife.

12. Decorate with grated chocolate or a pile of chocolate curls.

The cake keeps moist and gooey for 3-4 days.

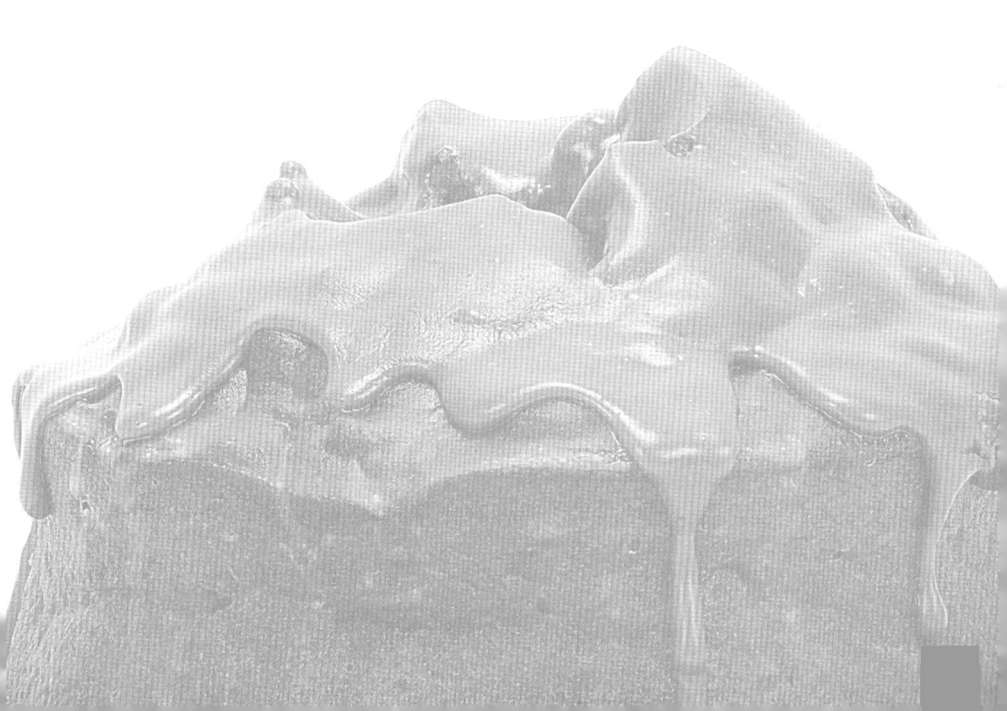

## Banana Cake

Preparation time: 45 minutes
Serves 6-8

### Ingredients

125g (4.5oz) soft margarine
4 tablespoons clear honey
2 ripe bananas, mashed plus 1 banana mashed with 1 teaspoon lemon juice
2 medium size eggs
125g (4.5oz) plain wholemeal flour
2 teaspoons baking powder, sifted
50g (2oz) curd cheese
2 teaspoons ground almonds
1 teaspoon clear honey

### Preparation

1. Grease and line two 18cm (7inch) sandwich tins.

2. Place the margarine, honey and bananas in a bowl and blend with a fork.

3. Add the eggs, flour and baking powder and beat together thoroughly until smooth.

4. Turn into the prepared tins and bake in a preheated oven, 180°C (350°F / Gas Mark 4) for 20-25 minutes until the cakes are springy to the touch. Cool on a wire rack.

5. To make the filling, mix the banana and lemon juice with the curd cheese, ground almonds and honey. Use to sandwich the cakes together.

This cake is best eaten within 48 hours.

# Scones

Preparation time: 30 minutes
Makes 6-8

## Ingredients

225g (8oz) self-raising flour
salt, to taste
1 teaspoon baking powder
2 tablespoons caster sugar (superfine granulated)
50g (2oz) butter
1 egg
120ml (4fl oz) milk
fresh double cream, to serve (heavy cream)
jam, of your choice
butter, to spread

## Preparation

1. Sift together the flour, salt and baking powder into a bowl and add the sugar and butter. Rub in the butter until the mixture resembles fine breadcrumbs.

2. Mix the egg and milk, then gradually add to the mixture to make a dough. Add your fruit at this stage as required.

3. Gently knead the dough on a lightly floured work surface until smooth.

4. Roll out the dough to about 1.5cm (1/2inch) thick, then cut out 5cm (2inch) rounds with a plain or fluted cutter, kneading and re-rolling the dough until it is all used up. Arrange scones on baking sheets then brush tops with milk.

5. Bake in the oven at 220°C (425°F / Gas Mark 7) for 8-10 minutes, until well risen and lightly golden. Cool on a wire rack.

6. Whip the fresh cream until stiff. Split the scones and fill with butter, jam and fresh cream.

## Welsh Cakes

Preparation time: 15 minutes
Makes 10

### Ingredients
450g (16oz) self-raising flour
100g (4oz) butter
pinch salt
100g (4oz) caster sugar
75g (3oz) sultanas
75g (3oz) currants
2 eggs

### Preparation
1. Sift the flour into a mixing bowl. Rub in butter finely.

2. Stir in salt, sugar, sultanas and currants. Make a well in the centre of the mixture and add beaten eggs. Mix to a fairly soft but not sticky dough, adding a little water if necessary.

3. Turn out onto a floured board and knead lightly until free from cracks.

4. Roll the mixture to 10mm (1/4inch) thickness and cut into rounds with a biscuit cutter.

5. Place on greased hot griddle or heavy frying pan and cook over moderate heat for about 5 minutes until golden brown on both sides and edges dry.

# Sunday Roast

## *Roast Chicken With Garlic, Rosemary & Lemon*

Preparation time: 20 minutes
Cooking time: 50 minutes
Serves 6-8

### Ingredients

1 whole chicken
250g (9oz) unsalted butter, softened
1 lemon
1 head garlic, peeled & minced
2 tablespoons chopped fresh rosemary
salt & freshly ground black pepper, to taste
1 teaspoon paprika
5 cloves garlic, sliced
5 sprigs fresh rosemary

### Preparation

1. Preheat oven to 180°C (350°F / Gas Mark 4).

2. Rinse the chicken and pat dry. Zest the lemon. Slice remaining lemon into quarters and set aside. With hand mixer, combine butter, lemon zest, minced garlic and chopped rosemary.

3. Take your hand and slide it between the skin and the meat on the breast, as well as loosening the 'pockets' between the leg and wing joints. Scoop some of the rosemary butter mixture onto your fingers and begin to stuff into the 'pockets' on the breast, leg, wings, etc. (Save approximately 1/4 of the rosemary butter mixture and rub on the inside of the chicken.)

4. Season the cavity of the chicken with the salt, pepper and paprika. Add the quartered lemon, rosemary sprigs and sliced garlic to the chicken cavity. Bind the legs with kitchen string and tuck the wings into the leg joints to secure.

## Roast Chicken With Garlic, Rosemary & Lemon/cont.

5. Place the chicken breast up onto a roasting tin and into the oven. Roast for approximately 50 minutes, or until the juices run clear.

6. Remove the 'stuffing', carve and serve.

## Roast Beef & Yorkshire Pudding

Preparation time: less than 30 minutes
Cooking time: 1-2 hours
Serves 4-8

### Ingredients
### For the Yorkshire pudding

350g (12oz) plain flour
4 large or 5 medium free-range eggs
800ml (7fl oz) milk
vegetable oil, for cooking
salt

### For the beef

2.5kg (45oz) oven-ready rib of beef on the bone
1 tablespoon English mustard powder
drizzle of vegetable oil or 2 teaspoon duck fat
freshly ground black pepper

### For the roast potatoes

16 medium-sized Maris Piper/King Edward potatoes (each about 175g (6oz))
8 garlic cloves
5 tablespoon duck fat
8 sprigs thyme
sea salt

### For the gravy

pan-roasting juices

# Sunday Roast

350ml (12fl oz) red wine
4 teaspoons plain flour

## Preparation

1. First make the Yorkshire pudding batter. Sift the flour and a pinch of salt into a bowl, add the eggs and gradually whisk in enough milk to make a smooth batter thick enough to coat the back of the spoon. Cover and leave to rest for six hours or overnight.

2. Preheat the oven to 200°C (400°F / Gas Mark 6). Take the beef out of the fridge and allow it to come back to room temperature.

3. Mix the mustard powder with a few teaspoons of water to make a paste. Rub the beef all over with the mustard paste and season well with salt and pepper.

4. Heat the oil or duck fat in a large frying pan. When hot, add the beef and sear on all sides, until it is nicely brown all over.

5. Place the beef in a roasting tin and roast in the oven for one hour (11 minutes per 450g (16oz) - this will give you rare meat). Cook for a further 15 minutes for medium-rare (14 minutes per 450g (16oz)) or a further 30 minutes for well-done (16 minutes per 450g (16oz)).

6. While the beef is cooking, prepare the roast potatoes. Peel the potatoes and parboil them in salted water for about seven minutes until almost cooked (they will still feel firm when pierced with a knife).

7. Drain thoroughly and then shake them around a little in the colander until the outsides are fluffy.

8. Remove the beef from the oven, transfer it to a carving board and cover with foil. Allow it to rest in a warm place for 30 minutes. Turn up the oven to 220°C (425°F / Gas Mark 7)

9. Put the duck fat for the roast potatoes into a small roasting tin and heat in

## Roast Beef & Yorkshire Pudding/cont.

the oven for five minutes. Add the potatoes to the tin with the garlic cloves, thyme and sea salt and toss them around until well coated in the fat. Return the tin to the oven and roast for 30-35 minutes until golden and crunchy.

10. Next make the Yorkshire puddings. Pour 5mm/1/2-inch of vegetable oil into the well of each Yorkshire pudding tin - eight individual ones or two four-hole trays. Place the tins in the oven to heat for a few minutes.

11. When the oil is hot, remove from the oven. Give the Yorkshire batter a stir and carefully pour it into the tins. Take care, as the oil may splatter. Fill each well up to about halfway.

12. Place the tins back in the oven and cook for about 25-30 minutes alongside the roast potatoes, until they are well risen and golden.

13. While the potatoes and Yorkshire puddings are in the oven, make the gravy. Place the tin with its roasting juices on the hob over a medium heat.

14. Stir in the flour and the red wine. Scrape well to get all the bits from the bottom of the tin into the gravy. Leave to simmer for ten minutes, then season.

15. To serve, carve the beef into thick slices and pile on plates with the Yorkshire puddings and roast potatoes. Pour lashings of gravy over the top.

## Roast Pork & Crackling

Preparation time: 30 minutes
Cooking time: 3 hours
Serves 6-8

### Ingredients

2.25kg (40oz) loin of pork, chined
1 small, onion peeled
1 tablespoon plain flour
275ml (10fl oz) dry cider

275ml (10fl oz) vegetable stock
sea salt & freshly milled black pepper

## Preparation

1. Pre-heat the oven to 200°C (400°F / Gas Mark 6).

2. Place the meat in the sink and pour over boiling water - then pat dry and sprinkle salt over skin.

3. Place the pork on a high shelf in the oven and roast it for 25 minutes. Turn the heat down to 200°C (400°F / Gas Mark 6), and calculate the total cooking time allowing 35 minutes per 450g (16oz). In this case it would be a further 2.5 hours.

4. To check to see when the pork is ready, insert a skewer in the thickest part and the juices that run out should be absolutely clear without any trace of pinkness.

5. When the pork is cooked remove it from the oven and give it at least 30 minutes resting time before carving. While that is happening, tilt the tin and spoon all the fat off, leaving only the juices. The onion should be black and charred, this gives the gravy a rich colour.

6. Leave the onion in, then place the roasting tin over direct heat, turned to low, sprinkle in the flour and quickly work it into the juices with a wooden spoon.

7. Now turn the heat up to medium and gradually add the cider and the stock, this time using a balloon whisk until it comes up to simmering point and you have a smooth rich gravy.

8. Taste and season with salt and pepper, then discard the onion and pour the gravy into a warmed serving jug. Serve the pork carved in slices with the crackling.

## *Roast Leg of Lamb*

Preparation time: less than 30 minutes
Cooking time: 1-2 hours
Serves 6-8

### Ingredients
### For the Lamb

1 leg of lamb, bone in, approx. 2kg (70oz)
4-5 garlic cloves, peeled
rosemary, freshly picked
salt & freshly ground black pepper
olive oil

### For the Roast Potatoes

1-1.5kg (36-54oz) roasting potatoes, peeled and cut into chunks.

### Preparation

1. Preheat the oven to 200°C (400°F / Gas Mark 6).

2. Using a sharp knife, prick the leg of lamb all over, about 20 times and about 2cm (1inch) deep.

3. Cut the garlic cloves into thin strips and place one slice of garlic into each hole with a few rosemary leaves. Continue until all the holes are full. Season with salt and freshly ground black pepper and drizzle with oil.

4. Place the lamb directly onto the oven rack and place a roasting tray directly underneath on the rack below. This is to catch the fat as it drips from the lamb. Roast in the pre-heated oven for 1 hour 15 minutes or until cooked to taste, basting frequently.

5. Parboil the potatoes. Drain them, then return them to the pan and shake to roughen the edges.

6. After the first 15-20 minutes of cooking the lamb, carefully tip the potatoes into

the roasting tray underneath the lamb, which will now contain the hot fat from the lamb above.

7. Coat the potatoes in the fat then roast with the lamb until golden and cooked through, turning once or twice.

## Beef Wellington

Preparation time: 30 minutes
Cooking time: 1 hour
Serves 8

### Ingredients

1.5kg (54oz) fillet of beef
375g (13 oz) puff pastry
225g (8 oz) button mushrooms
175g (6 oz) smooth liver pate
1 egg
40g (1.5oz) butter
1 tablespoon vegetable oil

### Preparation

1. Pre-heat oven to 220°C (425°F / Gas Mark 7).

2. Trim and tie up the beef at intervals with fine string so it retains its shape.

3. Heat the oil and 15g (1/2oz) of the butter in a large frying pan, add the beef and seal and lightly colour on all sides.

4. Roast for 20 minutes, allow the beef to cool then remove the string.

5. Fry the sliced mushrooms in the remaining butter until soft, allow to cool and mix with the pate.

6. On a lightly floured surface, roll out the pastry into a large rectangle to a thickness of 5mm (1/4inch).

## Beef Wellington/cont.

7. Spread the paté and mushroom mixture along the centre of the pastry. Place the meat on top in the centre.

8. Brush the edges of the pastry with the beaten egg. Fold the pastry edges over and turn over so that the join is underneath, folding the ends under the meat. Place on a baking tray and brush with the remaining egg.

9. Bake for 50-60 minutes, covering with foil after 25 minutes. Allow to rest for 10 minutes before serving.

## Honey Glazed Ham

Preparation time: 30 minutes
Cooking time: 2 hours 50 minutes
Serves 4-8

### Ingredients
### For the ham

2kg (70oz) smoked ham, with skin on
1 litre (32fl oz) dry cider
1 litre (32fl oz) water

### For the glaze

3 tablespoons honey
3 tablespoons wholegrain mustard
100ml (3fl oz) dry cider
handful cloves
1 tablespoon brown sugar

### Ingredients

1. Tie string around the ham to keep the meat in a compact shape as it cooks. Place in a large pan and cover with the water and cider. Cover with a lid and simmer for 2.5 hours, until the meat is tender.

Sunday Roast

2. Leave it to cool in the cooking liquid. Carefully cut the skin off the ham, making sure to leave the fat on. Criss-cross the fat with a sharp knife.

3. Preheat the oven to 220°C (425°F / Gas Mark 7)

4. For the glaze, warm the honey, sugar, mustard and cider in a pan and boil until it thickens to a treacle-like consistency. Spoon the glaze over the ham fat, and place in a roasting tin. Dot the cloves over the surface and bake for 20 minutes, or until the glaze has caramelised.

## Serving suggestion
Cut slices from the ham and serve with crusty bread, parsley sauce and peas.

## *Traditional Roast Turkey*
Preparation time: 30-45 minutes
Cooking time: various
Serves 6-8

## Ingredients
1 fresh turkey, or frozen turkey, defrosted
450g (16oz) fresh sausage meat
Melted butter or vegetable oil
Streaky bacon rashers
Salt & freshly ground black pepper
425ml (14fl oz) water
1 medium onion
1 carrot, quartered
1 bay leaf
6 black peppercorns
3 tablespoons plain flour, mixed to a smooth paste with cold water

You will need aluminium tin foil to cover the turkey with.

## Traditional Roast Turkey/cont.

### Preparation

1. Remove the giblets from the neck flap and the neck from the main cavity. Wash the turkey inside and out and pat dry with kitchen towel.

2. Loosen the skin at the neck end and remove the wishbone with a small, sharp knife to make carving easier. Spoon the sausage meat into the neck end, between the skin and breast, then tidy the neck skin by tucking it under the turkey to form a tight seal. Secure with a cocktail stick.

3. Any leftover sausage meat can be rolled into small balls and cooked separately. Weigh the turkey with the stuffing and calculate the cooking time, based on 45 minutes per 1 kg, plus 20 minutes.

4. Place the turkey on a wire rack which will fit into a large roasting tin. Brush liberally with melted butter or oil, then cover the breast with the bacon and season well with salt and pepper.

5. Pour the water into the roasting tin, add the onion, carrot, bay leaf, peppercorns and a little salt. Put the turkey on the rack over the roasting tin, cover loosely with aluminium foil and then place in a preheated oven 180°C (350°F / Gas Mark 4), for the calculated time.

6. Baste the turkey during cooking and add water if necessary. Remove the foil for the last 30 minutes of cooking if the turkey has not browned.

7. Check that it is cooked by piercing the thickest part of the thigh with a skewer. When the juices run clear the turkey is ready.

# Puddings

## Rice Pudding

Preparation time: 2 hours
Serves 4-6

### Ingredients

110g (4oz) pudding rice
410g (14oz) evaporated milk
570ml (18fl oz) whole milk
40g (2oz) golden granulated or caster sugar
2 tablespoons ground nutmeg
25g (1oz) butter

### Preparation

1. Preheat the oven to 150°C (300°F / Gas Mark 2)

2. You will also need a round ovenproof dish with a diameter of 23cm (9inch), 5cm (2inch) deep, lightly buttered.

3. Mix the evaporated milk and whole milk together, place the rice and sugar in the ovenproof dish, pour in the liquid and give it all a good stir.

4. Sprinkle the nutmeg all over the surface then, finally, dot the butter on top in little flecks.

5. Place the dish in the oven and leave for 30 minutes, take out and give everything a good stir. Repeat the stirring after a further 30 minutes, then pop the dish back in the oven to cook for another hour, this time without stirring.

6. At the end of this time the rice grains will have become swollen, with pools of creamy liquid all around them, and, of course, all that lovely skin!

7. Serve hot, with a dollop of strawberry jam.

## Bread Pudding

Preparation time: 2 hours
Cooking Time: 60-75 minutes
Serves 4-6

### Ingredients

225g (8oz) bread, white or brown, no crusts
275ml (9fl oz) milk
50g (2oz) butter, melted
75g (3oz) white or brown sugar
2 level teaspoons mixed spice
1 medium egg, beaten
175g (6oz) mixed fruit
grated rind of an orange
freshly grated nutmeg

### Preparation

1. Break the bread into suitable sized pieces and place in bowl. Pour over the milk, give the mixture a good stir and leave for at least 30 minutes.

2. Now add the melted butter, sugar, mixed spice and beaten egg. Using a fork, beat the mixture well.

3. Stir in the mixed fruit and orange rind.

4. Spread mixture in a prepared baking dish and sprinkle over grated nutmeg.

5. Preheat oven to 180°C (350°F / Gas Mark 4). Bake for about 60-75 minutes.

6. Serve hot with a dollop of vanilla ice-cream, or custard.

## Apple Pie & Custard

Preparation time: 20 minutes
Cooking Time: 40 minutes
Serves 6-8

## Ingredients
### For the pie
500g (18oz) shortcrust pastry
plain flour, for dusting
700g (25oz) cooking apples, peeled, cored & thickly sliced
pinch thyme
50g (2oz) caster sugar, plus extra for sprinkling
50g (2oz) soft brown sugar
25g (2oz) butter
1 egg, beaten

### For the custard
1 vanilla pod
300ml (10fl oz) milk
300ml (10fl oz) double cream
6 egg yolks
100g (4oz) caster sugar

## Preparation
1. Preheat the oven to 200°C (400°F / Gas Mark 6).

2. Roll out two thirds of the pastry on a floured work surface and use to line a 23cm (9inch) pie dish.

3. Tip the apple slices into a bowl with a pinch of thyme and the sugars, then stir gently to mix. Pile the mixture into the pastry-lined dish, dot with a little butter and leave to cool.

4. Once the filling has cooled, roll out the remaining pastry and lay it on top. Seal the edges well, then make a small hole in the top for steam to escape.

5. Make decorations from any pastry trimmings and seal them with a little water. Brush with beaten egg, sprinkle with caster sugar and bake for 20-30 minutes until golden brown.

## Apple Pie & Custard/cont.

6. For the custard, split open the vanilla pod and scrape out the seeds into a heavy-based saucepan. Pour in the milk and cream, add the vanilla pod, then bring slowly to the boil.

7. Whisk the egg yolks and sugar in a bowl until they lighten in colour and thicken slightly.

8. Pass the custard through a sieve, discarding the vanilla pod. Rinse the saucepan and return the mixture to the pan.

9. Put the saucepan over a low heat and cook the custard for 5-10 minutes, stirring all the time, until it thickens slightly and coats the back of the spoon - do not boil or the custard will curdle.

Serve with the hot apple pie.

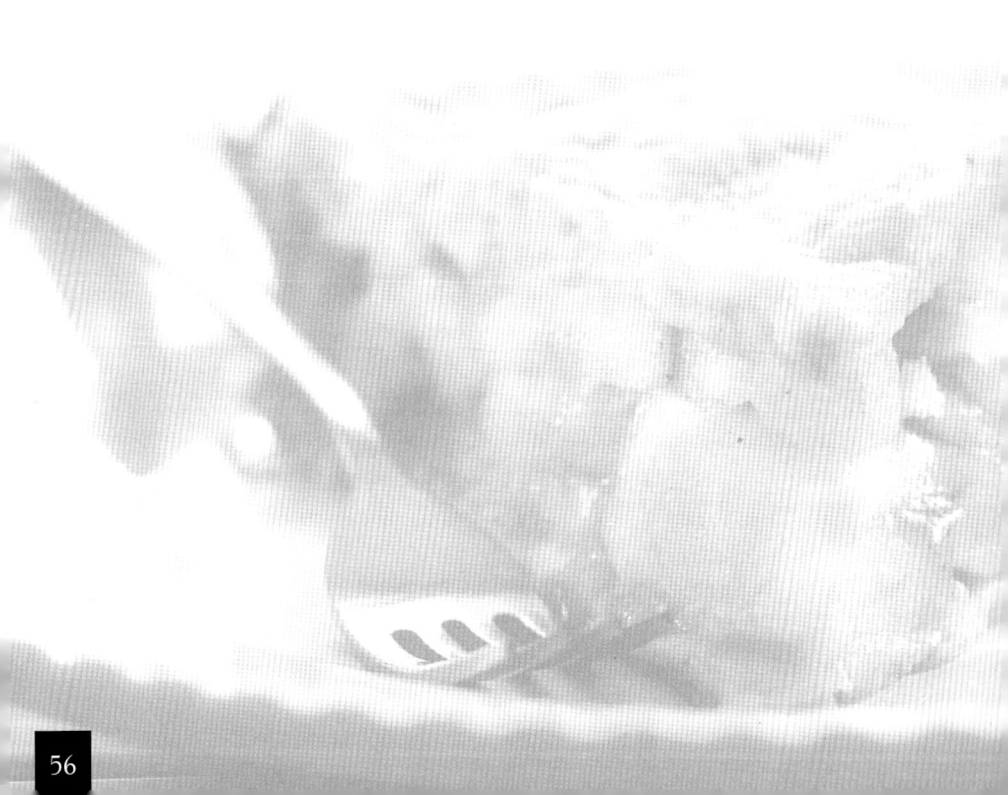

## English Pancakes

Preparation time: 10 minutes
Serves 4-6

### Ingredients
### For the pancake mixture
110g (4oz) plain flour, sifted
pinch of salt
2 eggs
200ml (7fl oz) milk mixed with 75ml (3fl oz) water
50g (2oz) butter

### To serve
caster sugar
lemon juice
lemon wedges

### Preparation

1. Sift the flour and salt into a mixing bowl with a sieve held high above the bowl.

2. Now make a hole in the centre of the flour and break the eggs into it.

3. Whisk the eggs, and gradually add small quantities of the milk and water mixture, still whisking (don't worry about any lumps as they will eventually disappear as you whisk).

4. When all the liquid has been added, use a spatula to scrape any bits of flour from around the edge into the centre, then whisk once more until the batter is smooth.

5. Now melt the butter in a pan. Spoon 2 tablespoons of the melted butter into the batter mix and whisk it in.

## *English Pancakes/cont.*

6. Get the pan really hot, then turn the heat down to a medium heat. Spoon the batter into a ladle so it can be poured into the hot pan in one go. As soon as the batter hits the hot pan, tip it around from side to side to get the base evenly coated with batter (it should take only half a minute or so to cook).

7. Flip the pancake over with a pan slice or palette knife - the other side will need a few seconds only - then simply slide it out of the pan onto a plate.

### Serving suggestion
To serve, sprinkle each pancake with lemon juice and caster sugar.

## *Spotted Dick*

Preparation time: 2 hours
Serves 4-6

### Ingredients
285g (10oz) self-raising flour
150g (5oz) shredded suet
150ml (5fl oz) milk
110-160g (4-6oz) currants or raisins
85g (3oz) caster sugar
1 lemon, zest only, finely grated
pinch salt

### Preparation

1. Mix all of the dry ingredients together, including the grated lemon zest,

2. Add enough milk to produce a soft dough. Turn out onto a floured surface.

3. Roll out the mixture to produce a roll approximately 15cm (6inch) long and 5cm (2inch) in diameter.

4. Prepare either a tea towel lightly dusted with flour, or sheet of kitchen foil or a double thickness of greaseproof paper, brushed with melted butter.

5. Wrap loosely but securely, leaving enough space for it to rise. Tie or seal the ends. Place in the steamer and cover tightly.

6. Steam for 1.5-2 hours. Serve cut into thick slices with hot custard.

## Custard Tart

Preparation time: 1.5 hours
Serves 6

### Ingredients
### For the pastry
175g (6oz) plain flour
pinch of salt
40g (2oz) of lard
40g (2oz) of butter

### For the filling
3 large eggs, plus 2 large egg yolks
570ml (18fl oz) single cream
50g (2oz) caster sugar
1/2 teaspoon vanilla extract
1.5 whole nutmegs, grated
1 level teaspoon of soft butter

### Preparation
1. Start by making the pastry. Sieve the flour into a large mixing bowl. Cut the butter and lard into cubes and add to the bowl with the salt.

2. Rub the butter and lard into the flour with your fingertips until crumbly and well incorporated. Sprinkle approximately 2 tablespoons of water all over the mixture and begin blending together with a pallet knife or round bladed knife.

## *Custard Tart/cont.*

3. Carefully add a little extra water if you feel the mixture is too dry but only a little at a time. Bring the dough together with your hands and mould into a ball that leaves the bowl clean. If you have any bits left in the bowl add a little more water to incorporate them.

4. Place the pastry in some cling film or foil and place in the fridge to rest for 20-30 minutes.

5. Preheat the oven to 200°C (400°F / Gas Mark 6) and place a baking sheet to warm on the centre shelf.

6. Roll out the pastry into a circle large enough for the pie dish or tin. Place the pastry into the dish and press down carefully to make sure it fits into the sides and bottom of the dish. Prick lightly all over with a fork.

7. Trim off the excess pastry from the edges of the dish with a knife. Brush the pastry all over with some beaten egg, and bake in the centre of the oven for 20 minutes until golden.

8. If the pastry rises in the middle prick again with a fork and press down carefully. When cooked, remove from the oven, leaving the baking sheet there.

9. Reduce the oven temperature to 160°C (325°F / Gas Mark 3).

10. Put the cream in a saucepan and heat until gently simmering. Gently beat the eggs and sugar together with a balloon whisk in a glass (heatproof) jug.

11. Pour the hot cream over the eggs and sugar and add the vanilla extract and half of the grated nutmeg. Whisk gently to incorporate all of the ingredients.

12. Put the pastry case back on the baking sheet and carefully pour in the custard mixture. Sprinkle the remainder of the nutmeg over the top and dot the butter over the surface and bake in the oven for 30-40 minutes until the filling is golden and slightly risen and firm in the centre. Serve hot or cold.

## Treacle Tart

Preparation time: 1 hour
Serves 4-6

### Ingredients
### For the pastry
225g (8oz) plain flour
110g (4oz) butter, chilled & diced
1 medium egg

### For the filling
450g (10oz) golden syrup
85g (3oz) fresh breadcrumbs
generous pinch ground ginger
1 lemon, zest, finely grated and 2 tablespoons of the juice

### Preparation

1. Rub the fat into the flour until it resembles fine breadcrumbs.

2. Mix in the egg with a knife, then knead to a smooth dough.

3. Use the dough to line a 23cm (9inch) loose bottomed tart tin, prick with a fork and leave to rest in the fridge for about 30 minutes.

4. Preheat the oven to 200°C (400°F / Gas Mark 6).

5. Bake the pastry for 10-15 minutes until light golden brown.

6. Mix together the filling ingredients and pour into the pastry case.

7. Bake for about 30 minutes. Serve hot or cold.

## *Trifle*

Preparation time: 30 minutes
Serves 4-6

### Ingredients

450g (16oz) sponge fingers (or jam swiss roll, sliced up)
25g (1oz) strawberry jam
tinned or fresh fruit (pears, peaches, pineapple)
35g (1.5oz) custard powder
350ml (12fl oz) milk, whole or skimmed
50g (2oz) caster sugar
120ml (4fl oz) cream (3/4 whipped) or non-dairy cream
235ml (8fl oz) whipped sweetened cream or non-dairy cream
25g (1oz) angelica
25g (1oz) glacé cherries

### Preparation

1. Cut the sponge in half, sideways, and spread with jam.

2. Place in a glass bowl and soak with fruit syrup or a few drops of sherry. Cut the fruit into small pieces and add to the sponge.

3. Mix the custard powder in a basin with some of the milk and add the sugar.

4. Bring the milk to boiling point, pour a little on the custard powder, mix well, return to the saucepan and over a low heat stir to the boil.

5. Allow to cool, stirring occasionally to prevent a skin forming, fold in the cream. Pour on to the sponge. Leave to cool.

6. Decorate with whipped cream, angelica and cherry.

## Puddings

## *Steamed Treacle Sponge Pudding*

Preparation time: 20 minutes
Cooking time: 2 hours
Serves 6-8

### Ingredients

3 tablespoons of golden syrup
175g (6oz) self-raising flour
1 rounded teaspoon of baking powder
175g (6oz) softened butter
3 large eggs
175g (6oz) soft light brown sugar

### You Will Need

1.2 litre (40fl oz) basin, well buttered
aluminium foil
greaseproof paper
string
steamer or large pan

### Preparation

1. Butter the basin, then add 3 tablespoons of golden syrup to the bottom. In a large mixing bowl, sift the flour and baking powder into it. Add the softened butter, sugar and eggs.

2. Whisk together with an electric hand whisk for around 2 minutes until it is well mixed. Spoon the mixture into the basin and smooth the top out with a large spoon.

3. Lay some greaseproof paper onto the work surface and the same size of foil on top of it. Be careful to ensure that you have it large enough to cover the top of the basin with extra to wrap around the sides. Form a pleat in both the paper and the foil together and place over the top of the basin with the foil uppermost.

4. Carefully smooth the foil and paper down around the basin and tie in place with some string. Form a "handle" of string over the top of the basin to enable you to

## *Steamed Treacle Sponge Pudding/cont.*
lift the basin in and out of the steamer.

5. Steam the pudding for 2 hours making sure to check the water level every 30 minutes to ensure that it doesn't boil dry.

6. Once cooking is complete, lift out the pudding and remove the foil and paper. Loosen the pudding all round using a palette knife. Place a large plate on top of the pudding and invert. Shake gently if necessary to release the pudding.

7. Lift off the basin with a cloth. Pour over another 3 tablespoons of warm golden syrup. Enjoy with custard or cream.

## *Heavenly Delight*
Preparation time: 20 minutes
Serves 4-6

### Ingredients
3 tablespoons gelatine
3 tablespoons hot water
50g (2oz) chocolate
350ml (12fl oz) milk
2 tablespoons sugar
3 yolks of eggs
120ml (4fl oz) cream
essence of vanilla
1 tablespoon rum

### Preparation
1. Cut chocolate into small pieces, place in saucepan with milk and sugar, then boil for 5 minutes.

2. Pour the chocolate onto beaten egg yolks, return to heat and cook until it thickens. Leave to cool.

3. Dissolve the gelatine in hot water, add to the mixture. Add the vanilla and rum. When the mixture is thickening, fold in the whipped cream.

4. Place in a serving bowl or mould. Chill.

## *Bakewell Tart*

Preparation time: 1 hour 30 minutes
Serves 4-6

### Ingredients
### For the pastry

175g (6oz) plain flour
pinch of salt
40g (2oz) of lard
40g (2oz) of butter

### For the filling

50g (2oz) butter
50g (2oz) caster sugar
50g (2oz) ground almonds
1 egg
2-3 drops almond essence
raspberry jam

### Preparation

1. Preheat the oven to 190°C (375°F / Gas Mark 5).

2. Start by making the pastry. Sieve the flour into a large mixing bowl. Cut the butter and lard into cubes and add to the bowl with the salt.

3. Rub the butter and lard into the flour with your fingertips until crumbly and well incorporated. Sprinkle approximately 2 tablespoons of water all over the mixture and begin blending together with a pallet knife or round bladed knife.

## Bakewell Tart/cont.

4. Carefully add a little extra water if you feel the mixture is too dry but only a little at a time. Bring the dough together with your hands and mould into a ball that leaves the bowl clean. If you have any bits left in the bowl, add a little more water to incorporate them.

5. Place the pastry in some cling film or foil and place in the fridge to rest for 20-30 minutes.

6. In a bowl, mix the butter and sugar together until creamy and well combined. Stir in the egg and then add the ground almonds and almond essence. Mix well to ensure all of the ingredients are well combined.

7. Spread a good layer of raspberry jam over the pastry base and spread the filling mixture over the pastry base and bake in the oven for 40 minutes.

8. Serve hot or cold with custard or cream.

## Blackberry & Apple Crumble

Preparation time: 60 minutes
Serves 4-6

### Ingredients
### For the Crumble

225g (8oz) plain or wholewheat flour
75g (3oz) butter (room temperature)
100g (4oz) soft brown sugar (to taste)

### For the Filling

600g (22oz) cooking apples
300g (11oz) blackberries
25g (1oz) soft brown sugar
2 tablespoons of water

## Preparation

1. Preheat the oven to 180°C (350°F / Gas Mark 4).

2. Core, peel and slice the apples and place in a saucepan with the water and sugar. Cook gently until the apples are soft. Put the cooked apples into a 1.75 litre (56fl oz) casserole dish and prepare the crumble topping.

3. Rinse the blackberries and mix gently with the cooked apples when ready.

4. Put the flour into a large mixing bowl and add the butter. Rub the flour and butter together until it looks crumbly and the butter has been evenly dispersed through the flour.

5. Add the sugar and mix together to ensure that everything is combined.

6. Sprinkle the crumble topping evenly over the top the cooked apples and blackberries using a fork to even out the distribution but don't press it down.

7. Cook in the oven for 30-40 minutes until lightly golden brown.

## *Sticky Toffee Pudding*

Preparation time: 40 minutes
Serves 6-8

### Ingredients

150g (5oz) pitted dates, chopped
250ml (8fl oz) water
2 teaspoons bicarbonate of soda
75g (3oz) unsalted butter, diced
125g (4.5oz) light muscovado sugar
2 medium eggs
2 tablespoons golden syrup
1 teaspoon vanilla extract
200g (7oz) plain flour

## Sticky Toffee Pudding/cont.

### For the sauce
100g (4oz) dark muscovado sugar
100g (4oz) unsalted butter
150ml (5fl oz) double cream

### Preparation
1. Preheat the oven to 190°C (375°F / Gas Mark 5) and butter a 18x27cm (7x11inch) baking tray or cake tin.

2. Bring the dates and the water to the boil in a small pan and simmer over a low heat for 5 minutes. Remove from the heat and stir in the bicarbonate of soda which will froth up.

3. Cream the butter and sugar together, add the eggs one at a time then add the syrup, vanilla extract and flour. Transfer the mixture to a large bowl and beat in the date mixture.

4. Pour the mixture into the tin and bake for 25 minutes until the top is set, the cake is risen and shrinking from the sides.

5. To make the sauce, heat the sugar, butter and cream together in a small pan whisking until smooth. Pour half the sauce over the cake and serve the remaining sauce separately.

# Sauces

## Fresh Mayonnaise
Preparation time: 15 minutes
Makes approximately 250ml (8fl oz)

### Ingredients
2 medium size egg yolks
1 teaspoon Dijon mustard
2 tablespoons white vinegar or more to taste
240ml (8fl oz) olive oil
freshly ground black pepper

### Preparation
1. In a small bowl, beat the egg yolks, mustard, a tablespoon of the vinegar, and a little pepper with a whisk until slightly thick.

2. Whisking constantly, beat in the oil drop by drop. After about 2 tablespoons of the oil have been added and the mayonnaise has started to thicken, add the oil in a thin, steady stream, beating constantly. Season with more vinegar and pepper to taste.

3. Prepare in a mixer, food processor or blender. Combine the egg yolks, mustard, a tablespoon of the vinegar and a little pepper in the bowl of the machine.

4. Turn on the machine and add the oil in a slow, steady stream.

5. If the finished mayonnaise is too thick, thin it with a little warm water.

## *Bechamel Sauce*

Preparation time: 30 minutes
Makes approximately 550ml (18fl oz)

This is the classic way of making a white sauce, using a mixture of butter and flour that the French call a roux.

## Ingredients

450ml (15fl oz) milk
a few parsley stalks
1 bay leaf
10 whole black peppercorns
1 slice onion, 5mm (1/4inch) thick
40g (2oz) butter
20g (1oz) plain flour
salt & freshly ground black pepper

## Preparation

1. First, place the milk in a small saucepan and add the parsley stalks, bay leaf, peppercorns and onion. Then place it over a low heat and let it come very slowly up to simmering point, which will take approximately 5 minutes.

2. Then remove the saucepan from the heat and strain the milk into a jug, discarding the flavourings.

3. All this can be done ahead of time, but when you want to make the sauce, use the same washed pan and place it over a gentle heat. Begin by melting the butter gently - don't overheat it or let it brown, as this will affect the colour and flavour of the sauce.

4. As soon as the butter melts, add the flour and, over a medium heat and using a small pointed wooden spoon, stir quite vigorously to make a smooth, glossy paste. Now begin adding the infused milk a little at a time - about 25ml (1fl oz) first of all and stir again vigorously.

5. Then, when this milk is incorporated, add the next amount and continue incorporating each bit of liquid before you add the next. When about half the milk is in, switch to a balloon whisk and start adding large amounts of milk, but always whisking briskly. Your reward will be a smooth, glossy, creamy sauce.

6. Now turn the heat down to its lowest setting and let the sauce cook for 5 minutes, whisking from time to time. While that's happening, taste and season with salt and freshly ground black pepper.

7. If you wish to keep the sauce warm, all you do is pour it into a warmed jug and cover the surface with clingfilm to stop a skin from forming, then place the jug in a pan of barely simmering water.

## *Traditional Gravy*

Preparation time: 15 minutes
Makes approximately 600ml (20fl oz)

### Ingredients

meat juices
2 tablespoons liquid meat fat
30g (1oz) plain flour
570ml (18fl oz) stock
2 teaspoons gravy browning (optional)

### Preparation

1. Collect the juices and the fat from the meat you are roasting. Put the juices in a glass jug and allow to stand for a few minutes so that the fat will rise to the surface. Skim off the fat.

2. Put the roasting tin that you used to cook the meat on the hob on a medium heat and add the fat. (The meat needs to be resting, covered with foil, in a warm place at this point).

3. Stir in the flour and cook for 1 minute.

## Traditional Gravy/cont.

4. Stir in the meat juices and gradually stir in the stock until you get a smooth gravy. Use a wooden spoon and stir all over the surface of the pan to incorporate any meat juices that are stuck to it.

5. Bring to the boil and allow to simmer for 10 minutes. Season to taste and add a little gravy browning if desired.

## Mint Sauce

Preparation time: 10 minutes
Makes approximately 35ml (1.5fl oz)

### Ingredients

25g (1oz) fresh mint, chopped
1 teaspoon caster sugar
1 tablespoon hot water
2 tablespoons white wine vinegar

### Preparation

1. Mix all the ingredients together and stand for 20 minutes to allow the mint flavour to develop.

## Horseradish Sauce

Preparation time: 10 minutes
Makes approximately 170ml (5.5fl oz)

### Ingredients

15g (1/2oz) freshly grated horseradish, soaked in 2 tablespoons hot water
1 tablespoon white wine vinegar
pinch of English mustard powder
pinch of caster sugar
salt & pepper to taste
150ml (5fl oz) double cream, lightly whipped

# Sauces

## Preparation

1. Drain the soaked horseradish and mix with all the other ingredients.

## Parsley Sauce

Preparation time: 10 minutes
Makes approximately 300ml (10fl oz)

### Ingredients

1 tablespoon butter
1 tablespoon flour
1 teaspoon minced garlic (or two cloves, chopped)
250ml (8fl oz) milk
seasoning to taste
2 tablespoons fresh parsley, chopped finely (or 1 tablespoon dried parsley)

### Preparation

1. Melt the butter in a saucepan. Add the garlic and let it cook over a low heat for 3 minutes.

2. Add the flour and seasoning and blend well.

3. Add the milk, little by little, stirring continuously until the sauce is thick and creamy.

4. Remove from heat and stir in the parsley.

## Cheese Sauce

Preparation time: 20 minutes
Makes approximately 800ml (28fl oz)

### Ingredients

40g (2oz) butter
40g (2oz) plain flour
600ml (20fl oz) milk
75g (3oz) grated Cheddar cheese
25g (1oz) grated Parmesan cheese
freshly ground black pepper

### Preparation

1. Melt the butter in a saucepan and stir in the flour to form a roux. Cook, stirring for 1 minute.

2. Remove the pan from the heat and stir in the milk. Return the pan to the heat & bring to the boil, stirring until thickened. Reduce the heat to a simmer and cook for 2 minutes.

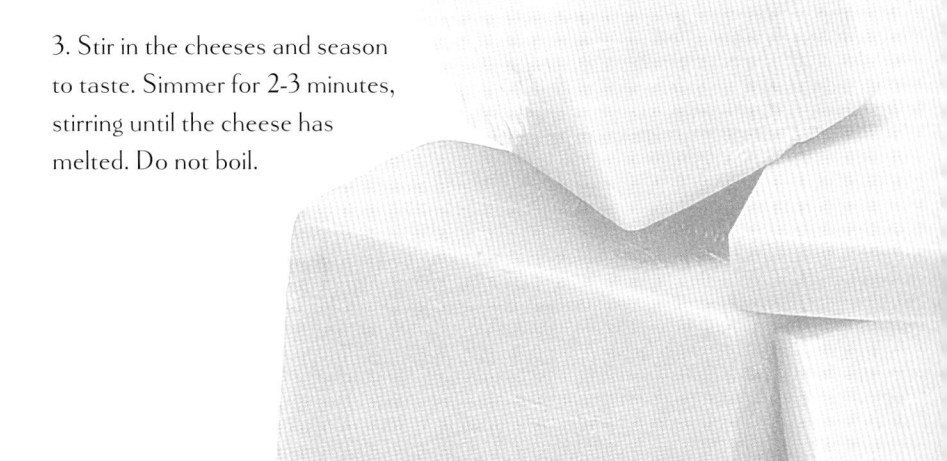

3. Stir in the cheeses and season to taste. Simmer for 2-3 minutes, stirring until the cheese has melted. Do not boil.

## Sauces

## Chocolate Sauce

Preparation time: 15 minutes
Makes approximately 210ml (7fl oz)

### Ingredients

50g (2oz) plain chocolate, grated
150ml (5fl oz) water
2 tablespoons golden syrup
2 tablespoons light brown sugar
1 teaspoon rum

### Preparation

1. Put the chocolate in a small heavy-based saucepan with the water, syrup and sugar. Heat gently to melt the chocolate and dissolve the sugar.

2. Once the sugar has dissolved, bring the mixture to the boil and cook for 30 seconds. Stir in the rum and serve hot or cold.

## Vegetable Stock

Preparation time: 45 minutes
Makes approximately 600ml (20fl oz)

### Ingredients

100g (4oz) each of a combination of uncooked vegetables such as cabbage, lettuce, broccoli, cauliflower, carrot, leeks & parsnips
6-8 whole peppercorns
1 bouquet garni
600ml water (20fl oz)

### Preparation

1. Place the washed vegetables in a large saucepan with the peppercorns & bouquet garni. Cover with the water and bring to the boil. Reduce the heat to a simmer and cook gently, uncovered for 30 minutes, skimming off any scum which rises to the top of the pan.

## Vegetable Stock/cont.

2. Strain the stock through a muslin or conical sieve, pressing the vegetables down well to remove all of the liquid.

3. Cool & store in the fridge, freeze or use immediately.

## Apple Sauce

Preparation time: 30 minutes
Makes approximately 475g (17oz)

### Ingredients

450g (16oz) cooking apples
25g (1oz) butter
1 tablespoon caster sugar
pinch of ginger

### Preparation

1. Peel, core and slice the apples and put in a heavy-based saucepan. Add 2-3 tablespoons water, cover and cook gently for 10-20 minutes until the apples have softened.

2. Rub the mixture through a sieve or blend to a purée in a food processor. Stir in the butter, sugar and pinch of ginger and serve hot or cold.

# Sauces

## Bearnaise Sauce

Preparation time: 30 minutes
Makes approximately 200ml (7fl oz)

### Ingredients

4 egg yolks
3 tablespoons white wine
3 tablespoons water
2 tablespoons white wine vinegar
1 teaspoon dried tarragon
100g (4oz) soft salted butter
3 shallots
bunch of fresh tarragon
freshly ground black pepper

### Preparation

1. Combine the shallots, pepper, dry tarragon and vinegar, and reduce very slowly to half the quantity then leave to cool.

2. Add the egg yolk and whisk thoroughly over a low heat until thickened. Add the diced butter and stir in thoroughly.

### Serving Suggestion

Add fresh tarragon and serve on the side of a prepared steak.

## Tartare Sauce

Preparation time: 10 minutes
Makes approximately 200ml (7fl oz)

### Ingredients

100ml (3.5fl oz) mayonnaise
1 shallot, very finely chopped
25g (1oz) gherkins, chopped
25g (1oz) capers, chopped

## *Tartare Sauce/cont.*

1 tablespoon parsley, chopped
1 hard-boiled egg, peeled & chopped
1-2 teaspoon lemon juice
freshly ground black pepper

### Preparation

1. Stir the shallot, gherkins, capers, parsley and hard-boiled egg into the sauce.

2. Season to taste with pepper and lemon juice.

## *Hollandaise Sauce*

Preparation time: 15 minutes
Makes approximately 200ml (7fl oz)

### Ingredients

3 tablespoons white wine vinegar
1 tablespoon water
4 peppercorns
1 bay leaf
3 egg yolks
175g (6oz) butter, softened

### Preparation

1. Boil the vinegar and water in a small saucepan with the peppercorns and bay leaf until it has reduced to 1 tablespoon of liquid. Leave to cool.

2. Cream the egg yolks with 15g (1/2oz) butter in a bowl. Strain the vinegar into the egg yolk mixture and place the bowl over a pan of hot water.

3. Turn off the heat and whisk in the remaining butter, a quarter at a time until the sauce is shiny and thick.

4. Season and serve immediately.

## Sauces

## *Bread Sauce*

Preparation time: 45 minutes
Makes approximately 400ml (13fl oz)

### Ingredients

1/2 onion
6 whole cloves
300ml (10fl oz) milk
1 bay leaf
1/4 teaspoon freshly grated nutmeg
75g (3oz) fresh white breadcrumbs
25g (1oz) butter
freshly ground white pepper

### Preparation

1. Peel the onion and stick the cloves into the flesh. Place in a saucepan with the milk and bay leaf, bring to scalding point, remove from the heat and infuse for 30 minutes.

2. Strain the milk into a clean saucepan, add the nutmeg, breadcrumbs and butter. Heat to scalding point over a very low heat. Do not allow it to boil as it may curdle.

3. Season to taste with pepper.

### Useful tip

It's often a good idea to make this in advance because if it appears a little thin at first, it can thicken on standing. Just reheat it when ready to serve.

## Beurre Blanc

Preparation time: 20 minutes
Makes approximately 150ml (5fl oz)

### Ingredients

1 shallot, finely chopped
5 tablespoons fish, chicken or vegetable stock
5 tablespoons dry white wine
1 tablespoon white wine vinegar
100g (4oz) unsalted butter
squeeze of lemon juice
ground white pepper

### Preparation

1. Cook the shallot in a little piece of the butter until soft. Add the stock, wine and vinegar, bring to the boil and simmer until it has reduced in quantity to about 3-4 tablespoons.

2. Keep the saucepan over the heat, but draw slightly to one side. Using a continuous whisking action, whisk in a little piece of the butter at a time until all is incorporated and the sauce has thickened. Do not allow the sauce to boil, but make sure that the sauce remains hot.

3. Season to taste with pepper and lemon juice.

# My Mum's Recipes

Ingredients

Preparation

# My Mum's Recipess

Ingredients

Preparation

# My Mum's Recipes

Ingredients

Preparation

# My Mum's Recipes

Ingredients

Preparation

Mum's Recipes

# My Mum's Recipes

Ingredients

Preparation

# My Mum's Recipes

Ingredients

Preparation

## Mum's Recipes

# My Mum's Recipes

Ingredients

Preparation

# My Mum's Recipes

Ingredients

Preparation

# My Mum's Recipes

Ingredients

Preparation

# My Mum's Recipes

Ingredients

Preparation

# Index

Apple Pie & Custard pp55-56
Apple Sauce pp76
Bakewell Tart pp65-66
Banana Cake pp40
Bearnaise Sauce pp77-78
Bechamel Sauce pp70-71
Beef & Ale Pie pp26-27
Beef Stroganoff pp28
Beef Wellington pp49-50
Beurre Blanc pp80
Blackberry & Apple Crumble pp66-67
Boiled Eggs pp1
Bread Pudding pp54
Bread Sauce pp79
Breakfast Muffin pp5-6
Bubble & Squeak pp23
Cauliflour Cheese pp21
Cheese & Potato Bake pp19-20
Cheese Sauce pp74
Chicken Chasseur pp27-28
Chilli Con Carne pp24-25
Chocolate Cake pp37-39
Chocolate Sauce pp75
Coggled Eggs pp3
Cornish Pasty pp18-19
Cottage Pie pp11-12
Custard Tart pp59-61
Eggs Benedict pp9-10
English Muffins pp6-7
English Pancakes pp57-59
Fish Pie pp16
Fresh Mayonnaise pp69
Fried Eggs pp1
Fruit Scones pp33
Fruity Porridge pp4

Gingerbread Man pp34
Heavenly Delight pp64-65
Hollandaise Sauce pp78
Honey Glazed Ham pp50-51
Hot Cross Buns pp29-30
Jam Roly Poly pp35-36
Kedgeree pp8-9
Lamb Hotpot pp16
Lamb Stew With Dumplings pp14-15
Lemon Drizzle Cake pp36-37
Luxury Toad in the Hole pp22
Mint Sauce pp72-73
Omelette With Crispy Bacon pp3-4
Parsley Sauce pp73
Roast Beef & Yorkshire Pudding pp44-46
Roast Chicken With Garlic, Rosemary & Lemon pp43-44
Roast Leg of Lamb pp48-49
Roast Pork & Crackling pp46-47
Rice Pudding pp53
Rock Cakes pp32-33
Scones pp41
Scrambled Eggs pp2
Steamed Treacle Sponge Pudding pp63-64
Sticky Toffee Pudding pp67-68
Traditional Gravy pp71-72
Traditional Roast Turkey pp51-52
Treacle Tart pp61
Trifle pp62
Vegetable Soup pp12-13
Vegetable Stock pp75-76
Victoria Sponge with Jam pp31-32
Welsh Cakes pp42
Welsh Rarebit pp20

# Index

## Spoons - Millilitres

| | | | |
|---|---|---|---|
| 1/2 teaspoon | 2.5ml | 1 tablespoon | 15ml |
| 1 teaspoon | 5ml | 2 tablespoons | 30ml |
| 1.5 teaspoons | 7.5ml | 3 tablespoons | 45ml |
| 2 teaspoons | 10ml | 4 tablespoons | 60ml |

## Grams - Ounces

| | | | |
|---|---|---|---|
| 10g | 0.25oz | 225g | 8oz |
| 15g | 0.38oz | 250g | 9oz |
| 25g | 1oz | 275g | 10oz |
| 50g | 2oz | 300g | 11oz |
| 75g | 3oz | 350g | 12oz |
| 110g | 4oz | 375g | 13oz |
| 150g | 5oz | 400g | 14oz |
| 175g | 6oz | 425g | 15oz |
| 200g | 7oz | 450g | 16oz |

## Metric - Cups

| | | |
|---|---|---|
| flour | 115g | 1 cup |
| honey | 350g | 1 cup |
| liquids | 225ml | 1 cup |

## Liquid Measures

| | | |
|---|---|---|
| 5fl oz | 1/4 pint | 150ml |
| 7.5fl oz | | 215ml |
| 10fl oz | 1/2 pint | 275ml |
| 15fl oz | | 425ml |
| 20fl oz | 1 pint | 570ml |
| 35fl oz | 1.75 pints | 1 litre |

## *Temperatures*

| Celcius | Farenheit | Gas Mark | Description |
| --- | --- | --- | --- |
| 110°C | 225°F | 1/4 | very cool |
| 130°C | 250°F | 1/2 | very cool |
| 140°C | 275°F | 1 | cool |
| 150°C | 300°F | 2 | cool |
| 170°C | 325°F | 3 | very moderate |
| 180°C | 350°F | 4 | moderate |
| 190°C | 375°F | 5 | moderate |
| 200°C | 400°F | 6 | moderately hot |
| 220°C | 425°F | 7 | hot |
| 230°C | 450°F | 8 | hot |
| 240°C | 475°F | 9 | very hot |